"From Pocket Money to Millionaire: The Secret to Smart Money Management" is perfect for anyone looking to understand how to handle money and take control of their future!"

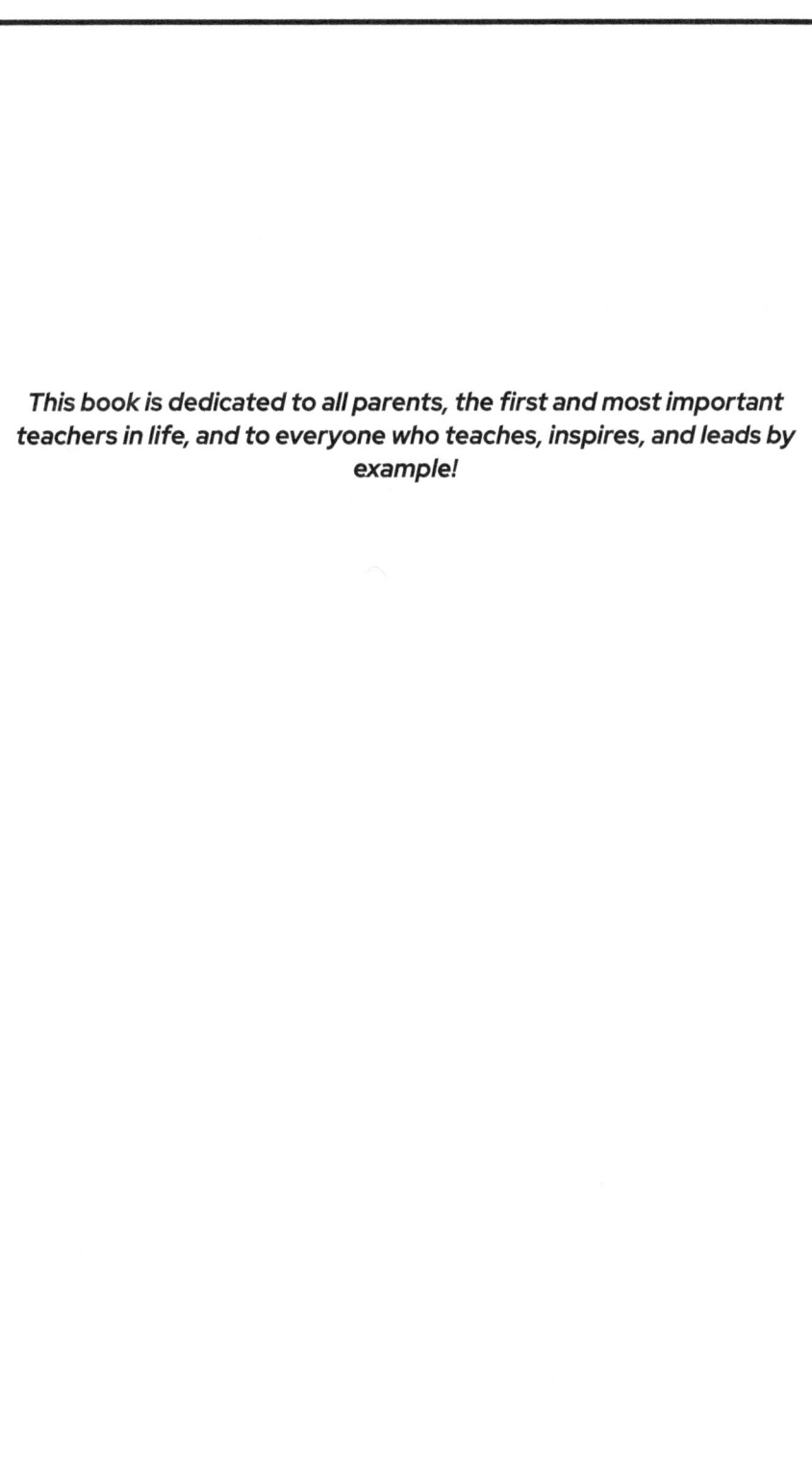

This book is dedicated to all parents, the first and most important teachers in life, and to everyone who teaches, inspires, and leads by example!

Acknowledgments

I want to thank my incredible wife, Erika—my best friend, my partner, my world, and my greatest support in everything I do. You complete my life and give me a reason every day to be the best I can be. This journey wouldn't have been the same without you.

This book is dedicated to my amazing children, Shyloh and Elijah. You're my inspiration and motivation, and everything I do is with you in mind. I'm also deeply grateful to my bonus children, Dylan and Kyara, who've become a cherished part of my life. This book is for you—to give you a strong foundation and the freedom to pursue your dreams. Your future is my pride, and my hope is that this book serves as a guide for a life full of opportunity, growth, and abundance.

Contents

Chapter 1

Lesson 1: Rich people don't work for money

The whole world works for money. The smart wealthy let money work for them.

Imagine waking up each morning with no worries about how much money you have and instead planning how to spend your day freely. No longer bound to a fixed salary or a job you dislike, nor stressed about money – sounds like a dream, right? For some, it's reality. Their secret? They understand something many don't: how to make money work for them, not the other way around.

Most people learn a lot about history, math, and geography in school. While valuable, there's a crucial subject left out: handling money. Wealthy individuals, however, learn that money is a tool you can use to lead a better life. This book is here to show you how to start building wealth for yourself, right now. No need to wait until you're an adult or have a "real" job. The first lesson to learn? The wealthy don't work for money.

Many think wealth is about working hard and earning a high salary. Parents, teachers, and society often tell us to get a good job to earn enough money. But what if becoming rich isn't about earning a salary at all? Wealthy people don't simply work harder to make more money; they work smarter to let money work for them.

In this chapter, we'll explore the difference between those who work for a paycheck and those who invest in assets – things that generate income, even if they're not actively working. You'll learn how today's choices impact your financial future. It's not just about how much you earn now; it's about how you use and grow that money.

Why Do People Work for Money?

Many believe working is the only way to earn money. They go from school to a job, save their wages, spend it, and then must return to work to earn more. This cycle, where people work, earn, spend, and then repeat, is a trap for many. This is what we call the circle, where many are stuck: working to earn, spending, and then needing to work again to earn more.

Consider someone with a job who receives a fixed paycheck each month. They work hard all month, receive their money, but it goes straight to bills, food, and perhaps a few new things they want. By the end of the month, the money is gone, and they must start over. They depend on their job to afford their life. This is what we call the rat race.

Look at yourself: what's the first thing you do when you get allowance or earn something from a part-time job? You probably spend it on something fun: new sneakers, a game, or maybe dinner with friends. That's understandable – you worked hard and want to treat yourself. The problem is, once you've spent it, the money's gone. It doesn't come back.

Wealthy people do things differently.

They let money work for them by buying things that make more money in the future. Instead of spending on new things, they invest in assets. Assets are things that can make money for you, like a small business, stocks, or something that increases in value. The more assets you have, the less you need to work for a salary.

The Difference Between Assets and Liabilities

One of the first lessons to learn is the difference between assets and liabilities. It may sound complicated, but it's simple. Assets make money for you, while liabilities cost you money. Think about a bike. A bike you buy to make deliveries and earn money is an asset. A bike you buy that only costs money for repairs and maintenance is a liability.

Wealthy people focus on buying assets. They want to own things that make money for them, so they won't need to work if they don't want to. Those who struggle financially often buy more liabilities: expensive cars, big houses, new phones. These things only cost money without giving anything back. The more liabilities you have, the more money you need to cover all the costs, which keeps you working nonstop.

The Circle of Money – How People Get Stuck

Let's talk about the cycle where many are trapped, also known as the rat race. Maybe you've seen a hamster running on a wheel without moving forward. That's what happens to people who spend their lives working for a paycheck. They keep running on that wheel but never make progress. They earn money, spend it, and then must work again to earn more. This goes on endlessly.

People go to school, learn a trade, and then find a job to earn money. They make money, spend it, and go back to work to earn more. This cycle can feel endless, leaving them with little time because they're always working to earn money. They're often too busy to consider how they could invest that money to make more.

Think of someone who spends their entire salary on a large car. That car costs a lot each month in fuel, insurance, and maintenance. To afford it, they must keep working, becoming more entangled in the work-and-spend cycle. The car doesn't make money for them; it only drains their finances. Wealthy people avoid such pitfalls, only buying things that cost money if they know it will ultimately help them earn more.

It's essential to realize that if you keep working for a salary and spending it directly on liabilities, true freedom may never come. Wealthy people know this and act differently. They make sure to buy assets so that their money works for them, not the other way around.

How Money Can Work for You

How can you make money work for you? It starts with buying assets. Imagine starting a small business, like selling handmade bracelets or offering dog-walking services. Once your business is set up, it can start earning money even if you're not constantly working on it. This is what we mean by "making money work for you."

Another example is investing in stocks. You might use some of your allowance to buy shares in a company you think will grow in value. As those shares appreciate, your money grows without extra effort from you. That's the power of compounding wealth.

The key takeaway is that you don't always have to work to make money. Once you acquire assets, they can help you earn more, even when you're not working. The goal is to make smart choices and invest in things that will help you grow your wealth over time.

The First Lesson: A First Job
Your first job can be a great experience, often marking the first time you earn your own money and feel a sense of responsibility. However, like many, you may find that earning a salary doesn't always bring fulfillment. You work hard but may feel stuck. This is a key moment to realize that working for a paycheck isn't the only path to success.

The real lesson here is that success isn't just about how much you earn but how you think about money. You can either work for wages, as most people do, or learn to make money work for you. This means shifting from merely exchanging time and effort for money to creating lasting value and thinking strategically. Instead of always working harder for a little more, ask yourself: how can I invest in myself and my future to grow my wealth without constantly working for it?

The Second Lesson: Learning About Money Is as Important as School
Schooling and good grades lay an essential foundation for your future, but there's another kind of knowledge that's equally important: financial literacy. While school prepares you for a career, financial education shows you how to manage the money you earn.

Many believe a degree is the key to success, yet even with a good salary, financial problems can arise if you don't know how to manage money. Without financial literacy, you're likely to overspend, leading to stress and debt. Understanding how money works, how to invest, and how to grow your income are critical skills. Learning about topics like investing, taxes, and entrepreneurship empowers you to take control of your financial future.

Lesson Three: What Rich People Do Differently
Rich people use their money differently than most people. While many people spend their money on things like a new phone, a car, or clothes, rich people use their money to invest in things that make more money. These are called assets—possessions that can increase in value or generate income.

Instead of spending your money on things you don't really need, learn to use your money wisely. Think about how you can invest in something that creates value, like a small business, stocks, or real estate. When you use your money to buy assets, you start building your future. This creates opportunities for your money to work for you, instead of you always having to work for money.

Lesson Four: Emotions and Money
Everyone has emotions around money. It can be tempting to immediately spend your money on things you like, like clothes or gadgets. Or you may be afraid to invest money because you see risks and are afraid of failure. These emotions are normal, but if you let fear or impulsiveness guide you, it can hold you back financially.

The key is to learn how to control your emotions when it comes to money. If you learn to manage risk and make smart, informed decisions, you can start investing and growing your money. It's important to remember that making mistakes is normal and that even wealthy people lose money sometimes. The difference is that they learn from their mistakes and come back better. The biggest mistake you can make is doing nothing because you're afraid of failing.

Lesson Five: The Importance of Independent Thinking

Many people follow the traditional path: school, a steady job, and hopefully one day enough money for retirement. But if you really want to be rich, you have to dare to think differently than most people. This means making your own choices, independent of what society tells you to do.

Instead of relying on a job and a paycheck, think about other ways to make money. Maybe you start a small business or invest in something you are passionate about. By thinking creatively and following your own path, you create opportunities that others may not see. This is how many successful people have built their wealth. They thought outside the box and dared to try something new.

Lesson Six: The Importance of Good Money Management

Finally, one of the most important lessons you can learn is how to manage your money. It doesn't matter how much you earn if you don't know how to use it wisely. This means that you need to learn to control your spending, save a portion of your income, and always look for ways to invest.

Creating a budget is one of the first steps. This gives you control over your spending and helps you avoid spending more than you earn. In addition, it is important to always set aside a portion of your income for investments. Even if it is a small amount at first, by investing wisely you can make your money grow.

The Lessons of This Chapter

When you apply the lessons of this first chapter to your life, you will see that getting rich is not about working hard for money. It is about using your money wisely, so that it can work for you. Rich people understand that you should not waste time and energy chasing a paycheck. Instead, they invest in assets, things that make money for them. You can do the same, by learning what assets are and how to buy them.

Remember: The goal is not to make more money by working harder. The goal is to make more money by working smarter. The sooner you learn this, the sooner you can start building your own financial freedom.

Chapter 1 Summary

In this first lesson of our book, we discover the fundamental difference between how wealthy people and most people manage money. Most people work for a paycheck, but wealthy people make their money work for them. While most people worry about making and spending money, wealthy people have learned that financial literacy and smart investments are the keys to wealth.

The chapter emphasizes the importance of assets—things that make money—as opposed to liabilities, which cost money. Wealthy people invest in assets such as businesses, real estate, and stocks, which allows them to become less dependent on a fixed paycheck and experience greater financial freedom. The cycle of working for money, also known as the "rat race," traps many people in an endless cycle of earning and spending. To escape this cycle, it is essential to manage money wisely and use it for investments that improve your financial future.

The chapter encourages readers to think differently about money, manage their spending, and recognize the value of financial education. Wealthy people develop a growth mindset and learn through mistakes, which helps them make better financial decisions and create opportunities.

Questionnaire

1. What is the difference between working for money and making money work for you?
2. What does it mean to be stuck in the "rat race"?
3. Can you give an example of an asset and a liability?
4. Why do wealthy people choose to buy assets instead of liabilities?
5. What happens when you spend your money on things that don't make you money?
6. How can starting a small business help you make money work for you?
7. What is the danger of always working for a paycheck and spending it right away?
8. How can investing in stocks make your money grow?
9. Why is financial freedom important, and how can you achieve it?
10. What action can you take now to start building your own assets?

This is just the beginning of your journey to financial freedom. In the next few chapters, we'll dive deeper into how you can make smarter financial choices and chart your own path to wealth.

Chapter 2
What Makes you a Millionaire: The Power of Passive Income

The rich focus on their possessions, While everyone else looks at how much money they have left to spend.

Passive income is money that you earn without having to work for it continuously. For example, this could be money that you earn by investing in something like real estate (which gives you rental income) or stocks (which give you dividends). The idea is that you make an investment once, and then that money keeps working for you, even when you're not actively working.

Why is this important?
Most people work for a salary, which means that they only earn money as long as they're working. But wealthy people understand that they have more freedom when they have income streams that keep flowing even when they're not working. Passive income gives you the opportunity to gain more financial freedom in the long run. It's like a money tap that, once properly installed, never stops flowing.

How can you apply this?
Even if you're young, you can start building passive income now. Even small investments can grow over time. Here are a few ways to get started:
- **Saving and investing:** If you save some of your allowance or side hustle, you can use that money to invest in something that will work for you in the long run, like stocks or index funds.
- **Starting a small business:** This can also generate passive income once it's up and running. For example, if you start an online store and sell products, the business can continue to make money even if you're not actively involved in it on a daily basis.
- **Online content:** If you're creative, you can create videos, music, or other content that earns money through advertising or sales even if you're not actively working.

How rich people earn passive income:
- **Investing in real estate:** They buy houses or apartments that they rent out and receive monthly income.

- **Stocks and dividends:** They buy shares in companies that pay out a portion of their profits (dividends) to shareholders.
- **Building businesses:** They start businesses that operate independently, so they generate income without having to be involved on a daily basis.

Lesson for you:
Building passive income takes time, but if you start now with small steps, you can achieve big results in the long run. Remember that your money should work for you, not the other way around. This way, you will slowly but surely build your financial future.

The Key to Passive Income: Assets and Liabilities
You may have heard the words "assets" and "liabilities" before, but what do they actually mean? Understanding what these words mean will help you on your journey to making your first million. This chapter will explore the difference between these two terms and why it's crucial to know what you're buying, especially if you want to get rich.

Many people think that wealth is simply about having a lot of money, but in reality, it's all about how you use that money. Rich people understand that you have to be smart about your purchases and always think long-term. They don't just focus on what they want now, but rather on what they can do to make their money grow in the future. The biggest difference between people who get rich and people who don't is that rich people buy assets instead of liabilities. But what exactly are assets and liabilities?

What is an Asset?
An asset is simply something that makes you money. It is a purchase that not only retains value, but also helps you make more money. It may sound complicated, but it is actually quite simple. Imagine you buy a bike to deliver meals. That bike makes you money, because you use it to work and generate income. In that case, that bike is an asset, because it helps you make more money than it costs.

Rich people invest their money in assets. They always think about how something can give them more value in the long run. This can be anything from a stock that increases in value to a company that makes a profit. Either way, the question always comes down to: "How can this make my money grow?"

What is a Liability?

A liability is the opposite of an asset. It is something that costs you money instead of making you money. Often, liabilities may seem useful or valuable at first glance, but they are ultimately a financial burden. Think of an expensive car for example. It may seem like a good idea to buy a nice new car, but that car costs you money. You have to pay for fuel, arrange insurance, and perform maintenance. It doesn't make you money, it sucks money out of your wallet.

A lot of people make the mistake of buying liabilities because they think that these purchases will make them richer. For example, they buy a big house or an expensive car because they think that it makes them look successful. But when you buy liabilities, you are just spending money without getting anything in return. That is exactly how many people stay in the "rat race."

Homeownership – Is It an Asset or Liability?

One of the biggest misconceptions about money is about buying your own home. Many people think that a home is an asset, but that is not always true. Your home can be a liability if you only use it to live in and it costs you money. You have to pay taxes, arrange insurance, make repairs, and much more. All of these costs mean that you are losing money instead of making it.

Of course, a home can become an asset if you rent it out and make an income from it. For example, if you rent out an extra room, that can make you money. Or if you buy a house that increases in value, you can sell it for more money later. But the main difference is that a house in itself is not automatically an asset, as many people think.

Rich people understand this and only buy houses if they know they can make money from it. Instead of spending a lot of money on a big house to live in, they invest in houses or apartments that they can rent out. This allows them to generate income and grow their wealth.

The middle class are the people who are somewhere in the middle when it comes to income and lifestyle. They earn enough to live comfortably, such as being able to afford a house, own a car, and go on vacation, but they are not super rich. They still have to work to pay their bills and do not have much extra money to invest in things like businesses or buy expensive things without worrying.

So, the middle class works hard to support themselves, but they do not have the freedom that rich people have, because they depend on their salary to get by.

This middle class will never become truly rich, despite having well-paying jobs. They spend most of their income on liabilities, such as houses, cars, and luxuries. They think that these assets make them rich, but in reality, they do not add much to their financial situation. They remain stuck in a cycle of working for their salary to pay their expenses.

You need to learn to invest your money in things that add value to your life instead of things that only add costs. This is one of the reasons why financial education is so important. Without this knowledge, people will continue to spend money on liabilities and will continue to rely on their jobs for their income.

What Makes You Rich?
Wealth isn't just about having a lot of money. It's about understanding how to make that money work for you. Many people think that they will become rich by simply earning more, but if you are only buying liabilities, that doesn't matter. The money you earn goes straight to things that don't make you money. Rich people, on the other hand, use their money to buy assets that make them more money.

Imagine this: you have two choices. You can spend your pocket money on a new game, or you can invest that money in a small business, like selling handmade bracelets. In the first case, you only get short-term enjoyment from the game, but in the second case, you earn money from your bracelets and can reinvest that money to make even more profit. That's the difference between buying liabilities and buying assets.

The Power of Your Choices
Every time you buy something, you are making a choice. You are choosing whether it will make you richer (assets) or poorer (liabilities). Of course, this does not mean that you should never buy something nice or that you should only think about the future. But if you want to be smart with your money and become rich, you have to know what you are doing with your money.

Every time you buy something, you can ask yourself: "Is this an asset or a liability?" If you invest money in something that adds value, something that will make you more money in the future, then you are making a smart choice. But if you spend your money on something that only costs money and does not yield anything, then you have to understand that too. You do not always have to make the perfect choice, but knowing what you are buying is an important step.

Choice exercise: Assets or Liabilities?
Let's do a little exercise. Imagine that you can buy these things with your pocket money or savings. Try to figure out which of these is an asset and which is a liability:
- A bike to deliver food.
- A fancy smartphone.
- Stocks in a company.
- A car that costs you a lot to maintain.
- A small online store to sell stuff.
- A gaming console.

Which of these purchases will make you money and which will just cost you money? Think carefully, because these are the choices you make every day in real life. Rich people buy assets, things that make them money. People who are stuck in the rat race buy liabilities and keep working to pay their bills.

Money Smart: What is it?
Money smart is the ability to understand financial data and situations and make smart decisions about money. This doesn't just mean knowing how much you earn or spend, but also understanding how to grow your money and how to manage financial risk. It involves learning to recognize good and bad investments, understanding how taxes work, and finding ways to make your money work for you.

Why is it important?
Many people think that you have to be rich to develop money knowledge, but in reality it is the other way around: you develop your money knowledge to become rich. People who are smart with money know how to manage their money and use it to build more wealth, while people without this knowledge are often stuck in the "rat race." They work for their money, spend it, and then have to start over without knowing how to get more out of their income.

How do you develop your money knowledge?
You start by learning about basics like saving, budgeting, and the difference between assets and liabilities. But that's just the beginning. You build your money knowledge by learning about investing, understanding different forms of income, and continually educating yourself about money. This can be done by reading books, watching videos, or simply starting with small investments and learning from them.

How do wealthy people use their money knowledge?
Rich people are distinguished by their ability to make smart decisions with their money. Instead of spending all their money on things that don't make them money, they use their money knowledge to buy assets that will make them more money in the long run. They also understand how to minimize risk through proper planning and research, and they continually learn how to improve their strategies.

Example: Let's say you have some money saved up and you have to make a choice: do you buy a new phone or do you invest that money in something that will make you more money in the future, like stocks or a small business? Knowledge of money teaches you that the phone is a liability (it costs you money) and the investment is an asset (it can make you more money in the future). By applying knowledge of money, you choose the investment and build your financial future.

Chapter 2 Summary

The Power of Passive Income Wealthy people focus on assets that make them money, while others often focus only on their expenses. Passive income is money you earn without working constantly, such as by investing in real estate or stocks. This type of income offers greater financial freedom because it continues even when you are not working. Even when you are young, you can start building passive income by saving, starting a small business, or creating online content.

Assets vs. Liabilities A crucial concept in building wealth is understanding assets and liabilities. Assets are things that generate money for you, such as a delivery bike or stocks that increase in value. Liabilities, on the other hand, are things that cost money without yielding any return, such as expensive cars or real estate that only has an expense.

Investing in Your Future A home is often considered an asset, but it can also be a liability if it only has an expense. Wealthy people invest in real estate that generates income, while the middle class often buys liabilities and is stuck in the "rat race." By investing in assets and being smart with money, you can secure your financial future.

Making Choices Every purchase is a choice that will make you richer or poorer. Being smart with money means understanding what you are buying and whether it is an asset or a liability. For example, investing in a small business can be more profitable than spending money on a video game. It is important to develop financial literacy and learn how to make your money grow.

Conclusion Wealth is not just based on how much money you have, but on how you use that money. By investing in assets and building financial literacy, you can improve your financial future and start the path to wealth.

Questionnaire

1. What is the difference between an asset and a liability?
2. Why is it important to buy assets if you want to get rich?
3. Can you always consider your own home as an asset? Why or why not?
4. Give an example of an asset that can make you money.
5. What happens to people who only buy liabilities?
6. Why can a bicycle be an asset if you use it to deliver meals?
7. What is an example of a liability that only costs you money?
8. How can you make your home an asset instead of a liability?
9. What does it mean to make your money "work for you"?
10. Which choice would you make: spend your money on a liability or invest it in an asset? Why?

In the next chapter, we will continue with how to buy your first assets and what are the best strategies to start investing in your financial future!

Lesson 3: Escaping The rat race

The rich work for freedom
Everyone else works for money

Everyone knows people who work hard, receive a salary every month, but are always short of money. You may recognize this in your own family or circle of friends. These people are trapped in what we call the "rat race": an endless cycle of working, earning money, and immediately spending that money on all kinds of obligations. It seems like they are starting over again and again, without really making any progress. This chapter is about how the rat race works, why so many people are stuck in it, and especially how you can escape.

What is the Rat Race?

The rat race is a situation in which people constantly work to earn money, but immediately spend that money on things that do not make them richer. For example, think of a job where you receive your salary every month, but that salary is immediately spent on rent or mortgage, bills, insurance, cars, groceries, and maybe a few nice things for yourself. And before you know it, the money is gone and you have to wait for the next salary payment.

In this way, many people remain stuck in the same cycle every month. They work hard, but at the end of the month they have nothing left to save or invest. That's how the rat race works: you keep running, but you don't get anywhere.

Why Do People Stay in the Rat Race?

The main reason people stay in the rat race is because they spend their money on liabilities instead of assets. A liability is something that costs money, while an asset makes money. People in the rat race spend their money on things that don't help them in the long run, such as expensive houses, cars, vacations, or gadgets. These purchases may seem fun or useful at the time, but in the end they are financial burdens. You have to keep working to pay for them.

The middle class stays poor because they keep investing in liabilities. They buy a house and see it as an investment, but forget that a house usually costs money: you have to pay taxes, maintain it, and pay interest on your mortgage. This keeps them trapped in the rat race.

On the other hand, rich people understand the difference between liabilities and assets very well. They make their money work for them by investing in assets such as businesses, stocks, or real estate that generate money. They don't spend all their money on things that only cost money. This allows them to be independent of a salary and gives them more freedom.

How the Rat Race Limits You

When you're stuck in the rat race, it may seem like you have control over your life because you have a paycheck and can pay your bills. But in reality, you're tied to your job. If you don't work for a month, you have no income and can't pay your bills. This is the big trap of the rat race: you work to pay off your debts, but you don't build up any wealth that can help you escape.

Many people feel like they're stuck in this cycle, and they are. They keep making the same mistakes over and over again, like buying expensive stuff they don't need or taking on huge debt for a big house. This traps them deeper and deeper into the rat race.

What makes this situation even more difficult is that it seems like this is the normal way of life. Many people think that all you have to do is work hard, buy a house, and save for retirement. But if you're not careful, you'll find yourself stuck in the same cycle when you're 60. This is exactly how the middle class continues to struggle with financial security, because they don't have a smart plan to build wealth.

How to Escape the Rat Race

The key to escaping the rat race is to develop a wealth mindset and focus on buying assets instead of liabilities. This means that you need to start investing your money in things that make you money, like stocks, owning a business, or real estate. This is how wealthy people make their money work for them.

Here are a few steps you can take to escape the rat race:
1. **Understand the difference between assets and liabilities:** If you don't understand this, you'll be stuck in the cycle of spending on

liabilities. Every time you want to buy something, take a moment to think: will this make me money in the long run (assets), or will it just cost me money (liabilities)?

2. **Invest in yourself:** Knowledge is one of the most powerful assets you can have. Learn about money, investing, and how to start a business. Understanding how to grow your money will help you make better choices.

3. **Invest your income in assets:** Don't just use your salary to buy liabilities like a car or gadgets, use it to buy assets. For example, instead of buying a new smartphone, you could invest that money in stocks or a business.

4. **Make a plan:** Rich people always have a plan for their money. They don't just spend money on things they don't need. You too can make a plan to invest a portion of your income each month in assets.

Choice exercise: Invest in assets or stay in the rat race?

Let's look at two scenarios:

- **Scenario 1:** Emma works full-time and buys an expensive car with her savings. She has to pay a lot each month for maintenance, gas, and insurance. Most of her salary goes to these costs and other bills. Emma continues to work to pay for the costs.

- **Scenario 2:** Jack works part-time and uses his savings to start a small online store. He sells handmade jewelry and earns extra money each month from the sales. Jack uses this money to further expand his business and increase his profits.

Which of these two is stuck in the rat race? And who is building assets to escape?

The difference between Emma and Jack is simple: Emma is buying a liability that costs her money, while Jack is building an asset that makes him money. This is the fundamental difference between staying in the rat race and the freedom to become financially independent.

Why Many People Stay in the Rat Race

Many people stay in the rat race because they are afraid to take risks. They choose security instead of investing in something that can make them money in the long run. This is often due to a lack of financial knowledge or a fear of making mistakes. But if you learn how to make smart investments, you don't have to be afraid. Taking risks is an essential part of building wealth.

Another reason is that people are **stuck in a conventional way of thinking**. They think that they just need a good job and work hard to achieve success. But as you have learned, this way of thinking keeps you trapped in the rat race. It is important to think differently and focus on how you can make your money work for you.

The Four Quadrants of Income (Cashflow Quadrant)
The Four Quadrants of Income divide the way people earn their money into four categories:
1. **Employee (E)** - You work for a boss and get paid a salary.
2. **Self-Employed (S)** - You work for yourself, for example as a freelancer or self-employed person.
3. **Entrepreneur (B)** - You have a company and other people work for you.
4. **Investor (I)** - You make your money work for you by investing in assets such as stocks, real estate or companies.

Why is it important?
Most people are in the **E** or **S** quadrant. They actively work for their money and depend on their work to have an income. Employees have a steady job, and self-employed people have to work constantly to keep their customers happy. Both quadrants have one thing in common: when you stop working, you stop earning. People in the **B** and I quadrants, on the other hand, have the opposite in common. Entrepreneurs have built systems or businesses that others work for, while investors invest their money in assets that generate profits even when they are not actively working. They are less dependent on their own labor and are better able to manage their time, which gives them much more freedom.

How can you move into the other quadrants?
It starts with developing financial intelligence and building assets. Working as an employee or self-employed is a great start, but if you want financial freedom, you need to learn how to move into the **B** and **I** quadrants. This means learning how to build a business, invest in assets that generate money for you, and eventually diversify your income streams so that you are no longer solely dependent on your own labor.

Example: Let's say you are currently a college student working as a cashier at a grocery store (you are in the **E** quadrant). If one day you decide to start an online store where you sell homemade products, you will move into the **B** quadrant, because you have set up a system that can generate profit independently of your work hours. Later, you can use the profit to invest in stocks or real estate, which will put you in the I quadrant, and thus create multiple streams of income.

The Power of Focus
Successful people focus on one clear goal and are not distracted by short-term temptations. This means that they use their energy and time for things that help them achieve their long-term goals, such as investing in themselves, their skills or their financial future.

Why is this important?
Many people are easily distracted by immediate gratification, such as impulsive purchases or time-wasting activities. Successful people, on the other hand, are able to focus on what is truly important. They set long-term goals and make conscious choices that help them achieve those goals, even if that means resisting certain short-term temptations.

How can you apply this?
As a teenager, you can harness the power of focus by directing your time and energy toward things that will help you grow, such as learning new skills, saving instead of spending money right away, and thinking about your future plans.

For example, instead of spending your allowance on a new gadget, you can choose to save or invest in something that will give you more long-term returns, such as starting a small business or taking a course. This is a way to shift your focus from what you want now to what you need in the long run.

The power of focus in action:
- Learn to prioritize: what will really help you achieve your goals?
- Avoid impulse buys: ask yourself if your purchase will help you in the long run.
- Focus on investing in yourself: how can you grow your skills or knowledge to be financially successful later?

By focusing on your financial future and keeping your goals clearly in mind, you can make better choices that will help you not only earn money, but also become financially free.

Chapter 3 Summary

In this chapter, you learned that the rat race is a dangerous trap that many people are trapped in. People stay poor because they spend their money on liabilities like expensive houses and cars, while not building any wealth. The middle class often stays trapped in this cycle because they think they can achieve wealth by earning more, but this doesn't work unless they invest their money in assets.

The Limitations of the Rat Race Working to pay off debt without building wealth limits freedom. This makes people feel like they have control over their lives, when in reality they are stuck in a vicious cycle.

Rich people understand this and buy assets that make them money. They make their money work for them, so they are not dependent on a paycheck. You too can escape the rat race by consciously choosing assets over liabilities, investing in yourself, and making a plan to build your financial future.

Escaping the Rat Race To escape the rat race, it's important to develop a wealth mindset and invest in assets. Some steps to escaping include:
- **Understand the difference between assets and liabilities:** Ask yourself if a purchase will make or cost you money in the long run.
- **Invest in yourself:** Learn about money and investments.
- **Put your income toward assets:** Use your salary to invest in assets instead of liabilities.
- **Create a financial plan:** Invest a portion of your income each month in assets.

The Four Quadrants of Income The four quadrants—Employee (E), Self-Employed (S), Entrepreneur (B), and Investor (I)—illustrate how people earn their money. Most people are in the E and S quadrants, where they rely on active work. To achieve financial freedom, they must move into the B and I quadrants.

The Power of Focus

Successful people set long-term goals and don't get distracted by short-term temptations. This is crucial for financial growth. Teens can apply this by saving and investing in their future instead of making impulsive purchases.

Applying Focus

- **Prioritize:** Identify what will help you achieve your goals.
- **Avoid impulsive purchases:** Ask yourself if the purchase will help you in the long run.
- **Focus on self-investment:** Expand your skills and knowledge for future financial success.

By applying these strategies, people can not only increase their income, but also achieve financial freedom and escape the rat race.

Questionnaire
1. What is the rat race?
2. Why does the middle class often get stuck in the rat race?
3. What is the main difference between assets and liabilities?
4. Give an example of a liability that costs you money.
5. How can you avoid getting stuck in the rat race?
6. What does Emma do wrong in the choice exercise scenario?
7. What does Jack do right in the choice exercise scenario?
8. Why is it important to invest in yourself if you want to get out of the rat race?
9. What does it mean to make your money work for you?
10. What steps can you take to start buying assets now?

In the next chapter, we will discuss how to buy your first assets and how to build your financial future the smart way!

Chapter 4

Lesson 4: Learning about money – Just as important as School

It's not about how much you make.
It's about how much you keep

In school, you learn all sorts of things: math, geography, language, history, and much more. All of these subjects are important to increase your general knowledge and prepare you for a degree or a job. But there is one important subject that is almost never covered: money. You may learn how to calculate percentages, but do you also know how to apply that knowledge to manage your money wisely? Did you know that understanding money, investing, and planning for money can be just as important as the subjects you learn in school?

In this chapter, we discuss why knowledge about money is essential, and why you don't always learn it in school. If you want to become rich or achieve financial freedom, it is important to build this knowledge. And the great thing is: you can start today.

Why Learning About Money Is So Important

Money plays an important role in almost everything we do. Whether you want to study, go on vacation, buy your own house, or just do your daily shopping, money is always necessary. But surprisingly, most people don't learn how to manage money properly until later in life—often after they've made mistakes and racked up debt.

That's because we don't learn much about personal finance in school. We learn complicated math formulas, but not how to budget or how to invest to make our money grow. This lack of knowledge about money is one of the main reasons why so many people struggle with money management.

Many adults admit to making mistakes with money because they simply didn't know any better. For example, they took on too much debt or spent their money on things that didn't benefit them in the long run. This is exactly why learning about money is as important as getting good grades in school: it can help you make better decisions and make your future more secure.

What You Don't Learn in School
While some schools cover basic things like saving or budgeting, most of the money topics that really matter are under-exposed. For example:

1. **Investing** – Did you know that you can make your money grow by investing it in stocks, bonds, or real estate? Many people don't learn this until they've been working for a long time, but if you start investing young, you can reap huge rewards from money.
2. **Taxes** – It may seem boring, but taxes are an important part of how our money works. Understanding how taxes work can help you avoid overpaying and even learn how to pay less tax by investing wisely.
3. **Entrepreneurship** – Many schools encourage you to work for a boss, but entrepreneurship can be a great way to take control of your income. Starting your own business offers opportunities to increase your income and gain freedom.
4. **Interest and debt** – Understanding how interest works can help you understand why it's dangerous to take on too much debt. High-interest debt can trap you, while smart borrowing can sometimes make you money.

Wealthy people understand these words well. They use this knowledge to make smart financial decisions. People who are less successful with money often never had the chance to learn these things – in school or at home. But you can choose to learn how money works now, so you don't have to make the same mistakes.

What Rich People Do Differently?
Rich people are not necessarily luckier than others, but they do have a better understanding of money. They understand that you not only have to work hard for your money, but that you also have to make your money work for you. They do this by investing in assets that will make them more money, as you learned in previous chapters.

Another important difference is that rich people spend a lot of time and effort learning about money. They read books, take courses, and talk to experts to understand how to improve their financial situation. Unlike most people, they don't just settle for what they know; they always want to learn more and expand their knowledge.

Think about it: How much time do you spend learning about money? Compare that to how much time you spend studying subjects like history or math. If you spent as much time learning about money as you do studying subjects, how would it change your financial future?

The Consequences of Not Knowing About Money

If you don't have good money knowledge, you run the risk of making mistakes that will haunt you for years. For example, many people get stuck in a life of debt because they don't understand how interest works. Others don't know how to grow their money through investments, and just keep their savings in a bank account where it loses value due to inflation.

One of the biggest dangers of not knowing about money is that it keeps you trapped in a life of limitations. Without the right knowledge, you'll stay stuck in a job because you can't afford other options. You'll spend your money on liabilities instead of assets, and you may struggle to build a good future for yourself or your family.

But if you learn how to manage money, you open a door to an almost unlimited flow of money. This means that you are in control of your life and your money works for you, instead of the other way around. You can choose what you do, instead of being forced to do things because you need money.

Your Choice: Learn About Money or Just Follow?

Now that you understand the importance of learning about money, you have a choice: will you take action and learn more about money? Or will you continue to focus on school subjects without learning more about money?

Both choices have consequences for your future. If you decide to learn more about money, for example by reading books, watching videos or taking courses, you will discover how to build wealth and invest wisely. This opens the door to a life where you are less dependent on a job or a paycheck.

On the other hand, if you don't make the extra effort to learn about money, you run the risk of getting stuck in the money constraints that so many people face. You may find yourself struggling later in life because you lack important knowledge about money.

Why Self-Education Is So Powerful

Fortunately, you can start learning about money even when you're young. There are many books, blogs, podcasts, and videos specifically geared toward learning the basics of finance. The sooner you start, the more you can benefit from this knowledge.

Self-education is one of the most powerful ways to develop yourself. You don't have to wait for school to teach you something. In fact, many successful entrepreneurs and investors have taught themselves how to be smart about money. They've taken the responsibility to learn more than what school could teach them.

Money Knowledge: Tax Benefits for the Rich

Wealthy people understand how tax laws work and use this knowledge to their advantage. They invest in assets like real estate or businesses, which often come with tax benefits. Instead of receiving all of their income as a salary (which is heavily taxed), they know how to invest their money in ways that are taxed less.

Why is this important?

When you earn money as an employee, you pay a fixed percentage of tax on your income. The more you earn, the more tax you pay. But wealthy people understand that by investing in certain assets, such as real estate, they can reduce their tax burden. Instead of earning money right away and paying taxes on it, they invest in assets that not only make them more money, but also offer tax benefits. This is an important strategy that helps them grow their wealth faster.

How does this work?

There are several ways that wealthy people take advantage of tax benefits. Here are a few examples:
- **Real estate investors** can get tax benefits such as depreciation (the decrease in value of a property over time), which reduces their tax bill.
- **Business owners** can get tax deductions for business expenses, such as payroll, rent, or investments in their business.
- **Investors** in stocks or other assets often pay a lower tax rate on profits (capital gains tax) than someone who receives wages, because this type of income is taxed at a lower rate.

These tax benefits help wealthy people grow their wealth without paying more and more taxes, which puts them ahead financially.

Why should this matter to you?
Understanding tax benefits can help you make smart investment choices in the future. If you learn how to invest your money wisely, such as in real estate or a business, you can not only grow your income but also pay less in taxes. This is one of the ways that wealthy people achieve financial freedom, and it's something you can learn to do too. I'll go into more detail about this in a future chapter.

Chapter 4 Summary

In this chapter, you learned why money knowledge is just as important as the subjects you learn in school. Although many schools pay little attention to money matters, it is essential to understand how to manage, invest, and grow your money. Without this knowledge, you risk getting stuck in money problems, such as debt or a lack of savings.

Wealthy people understand the power of money knowledge and spend a lot of time learning about it. By applying this knowledge, they can build their wealth and live their lives more freely. You too can start learning these skills, even outside of school.

What is not taught in school?

Many important topics, such as:
- **Investing**: How to grow your money by investing it in assets such as stocks and real estate.
- **Taxes**: The importance of tax knowledge to avoid overpaying and how smart investments can provide tax benefits.
- **Entrepreneurship**: The opportunities that arise when you take control of your income by starting your own business.
- **Interest and Debt:** Understanding interest helps you avoid falling into a debt trap.

Financial freedom begins with choosing to invest in yourself and learning how to use money to achieve your dreams. Start learning about money today and discover how you can create a better future for yourself.

Conclusion

It is essential to start learning about money early to build a solid financial foundation. By increasing your knowledge about money, you can make better choices, grow your wealth, and achieve financial freedom.

Questionnaire

1. Why is money knowledge important for your future?
2. What topics are not taught in school that are important for managing your money?
3. How do wealthy people use money knowledge to build their wealth?
4. Why do many people remain in financial trouble?
5. What are the benefits of learning about investments at a young age?
6. Why can not learning about money be dangerous for your future?
7. What does it mean to make your money work for you?
8. What role does self-education play in learning about money?
9. What would your life be like if you did not have good money knowledge?
10. What steps can you take today to learn more about money?

In the next chapter, we will discuss how you can start building your own financial foundation and take the first steps towards investing!

Lesson 5: Work to learn, Not to make money

<u>Job security means everything to parents.</u>
<u>Education means everything to the rich.</u>

When you're young and starting out in the workforce, it's tempting to think that making money is the most important thing. Maybe you want to make money fast to do fun things like travel, go out, or buy new gadgets. But did you know that wealthy people think differently about their first jobs and careers? For them, the real value of work isn't the salary you get, but the knowledge and skills you gain. Instead of working just for the money, they see work as an opportunity to learn, grow, and prepare themselves for the future.

This chapter is about why learning is more important than making money in your early career. It's about focusing on developing skills and building experience that can pay off much more later than a higher salary now. Instead of thinking of work as a way to make money, think of it as an investment in yourself.

Why Learning Is More Important Than Earning
In your early career, the experience you gain is much more valuable than the money you earn. Think about it: A high salary may be tempting, but what good is that money if you don't know what to do with it later? Rich people understand that knowledge and skills can ultimately earn you more money than a high salary early in their career. This is because skills and knowledge can snowball and become more valuable as you learn more.

Here are a few reasons why you should focus on learning instead of earning:
1. **Long-Term Benefits** – The skills you learn now can help you earn more money or get better opportunities later. For example, if you learn how a business works now, you can use that knowledge later to start your own business or move up in another company.
2. **Networking** – When you work to learn, you often meet people who can share valuable insights or help you with your future plans. These

connections can be much more valuable than your salary because they can open doors to new opportunities.

3. **Versatility** – When you focus on learning, you often learn a wider variety of things than if you just did a specific task for money. This helps you become more versatile and perform well in multiple areas, which creates more opportunities in the future.

4. **Personal Development** – Working to learn also gives you the opportunity to grow personally. You may learn things about leadership, perseverance, and problem solving that you can use for the rest of your life.

Wealthy People Use Work to Learn

Wealthy and successful people understand that the primary goal of working is not the paycheck, but the experience. They often choose jobs or internships that teach them about things like finance, entrepreneurship, or management, even if these jobs don't pay well. They know that the knowledge they gain can help them make more money later than a high salary would now.

For example, a successful entrepreneur might start as an intern in a company where he or she learns everything about how the company works. The intern may not make much money, but the experience is priceless. They learn how to run a business, how to attract customers, how to handle finances, and more. Later, they can use this knowledge to build their own successful business, something that is worth much more than that small salary in the beginning.

What Job Should You Choose?

Instead of choosing a job that will pay you the most, consider choosing a job that will give you the most knowledge and experience. Maybe this means choosing an internship that teaches you about finance, even if it doesn't pay well. Or maybe you choose a job in a startup, where you are more involved in different aspects of the business, instead of a large company where you might have a small, specialized task.

Here are some examples of jobs and experiences that can teach you a lot, even if they don't pay very well:

1. **Internships at a company** – This gives you the chance to see how a company works from the inside. You'll learn about the structure of companies, how decisions are made, and how finances work.

2. **Working at a small business or startup** – In a small business, you'll often have the opportunity to work in multiple roles. This helps you develop different skills and learn how a company really works.
3. **Jobs that require sales skills** – Sales experience can be invaluable. You'll learn how to communicate with people, how to sell yourself and your ideas, and how to persuade people – all skills you can use later in your career.
4. **Volunteer work or projects** – Even though you don't get paid for it, volunteer work can give you the chance to gain valuable experience and build a network.

The Power of Learning from Experience

Working to learn isn't always easy. Sometimes it can feel like you're not making much progress or that you're earning less than your friends. But remember that the value of the knowledge and experience you gain extends far beyond your current salary. These skills can make the difference later in life between someone who knows little about money and someone who can create their own future.

Every new experience you gain is like a piece of a puzzle. The more pieces you collect, the more complete the picture becomes. And the more complete that picture, the better prepared you are for the future. Unlike money, which you can spend and lose, knowledge and experience stay with you forever and only become more valuable.

Your Choice: Money or Experience?

Now that you know this, you have an important choice to make. Do you go for a well-paid job that doesn't teach you much? Or do you go for a job or internship that may pay you less but will teach you important skills? Think carefully about the long term: which will pay you more in the future?

If you choose a well-paid job now, you may get an immediate financial advantage. But you may miss out on the opportunity to learn valuable lessons that could pay you much more later.

On the other hand, when you choose a learning experience, you are investing in yourself and your future. You are building skills that you can use later in your career to achieve greater success, make more money, or even start your own business.

Leadership and Teamwork

Rich people understand that they don't have to do everything alone. They surround themselves with experts who can help them make the best financial decisions. They build teams of specialists, such as accountants, lawyers, and financial advisors, to support them. This allows them to be better informed, make smarter choices, and minimize risk.

Why is this important?

The idea that you have to do everything yourself can be limiting. Rich people know that success often comes from good teamwork and trusting people who know more about certain topics. They work with experts who can help them develop the best financial strategies, which is crucial to getting ahead financially.

Here are some examples of people who have rich people on their teams:
- **Accountants** help manage cash flows and maximize tax benefits.
- **Lawyers** make sure that their investments and businesses are legally protected.
- **Financial advisors** help you choose the best investments and build long-term plans.

This means that getting rich isn't about doing it all yourself, but about building a good team around you that helps you be better informed and make more efficient decisions.

How can this work for you?

You can apply this lesson by recognizing that you don't have to know or be able to do everything to be successful. By getting help from experts or people who are more knowledgeable about a particular topic, you can make smarter choices with your money and better plan your financial future.

Even as a teenager, you can embrace this principle by asking your parents, teachers, or mentors for advice when making financial decisions. The more you learn from others, the better you will become at managing your money and making good choices.

Lesson: Invest in Yourself

The most important thing you can do in your early career is invest in yourself. This means taking the time to learn, grow, and gain skills that will help you in the future. By viewing work as an opportunity to learn, you set yourself up for long-term success.

Of course, it is important to earn money to provide for your basic needs, but it is crucial to choose work that teaches you something. Look for opportunities where you can grow, even if that means earning a little less now. The value of the knowledge you gain is ultimately much greater than any salary. And remember: you certainly don't have to do it alone! Find people around you who can help you become smarter with money.

Chapter 5 Summary
In this chapter, you learned that early career work shouldn't just be about making money, but about learning new skills and gaining experience. Wealthy people know that the knowledge you gain can be far more valuable than a high salary in the beginning. By working to learn, you prepare yourself for the future and build a strong foundation for financial success.

You also learned that you have the choice to work for money or for experience. By choosing work that builds your skills, you are investing in yourself and your future success.

Why Learning is More Important Than Earning
- **Long-Term Benefits:** The skills you learn now will help you achieve better career opportunities and higher incomes later.
- **Networking:** By working to learn, you will meet valuable contacts who can help you in your future.
- **Versatility:** Learning in a variety of areas will increase your opportunities in the future.
- **Personal Development:** You will develop invaluable skills such as leadership and problem-solving.

Wealthy People Use Work to Learn
Wealthy and successful people focus on gaining experience in their early jobs, even if the pay is limited financially. They often choose positions or internships that teach them valuable lessons about finance, business, or management. This knowledge provides a solid foundation for future success.

What Job Should You Choose?
Rather than opting for the highest pay, choose work that offers you the most knowledge and experience. Some suggestions include:
- **Internship at a company:** Learn the inner workings of an organization.

- **Work at a small business or startup:** Get the chance to play a variety of roles.
- **Sales experience:** Develop communication skills that will benefit you later.
- **Volunteer work:** This provides valuable experience and the opportunity to build a network.

Lesson: Invest in Yourself

The most important thing in your early career is to invest in yourself by gaining skills and knowledge. Look for opportunities to grow, even if it means making less money now. The value of this knowledge and experience will ultimately be far greater than any salary. Also seek the help of others to guide you in the process of learning and growing.

Questionnaire

1. Why is learning more important in your early career than making money?
2. What kinds of experiences can pay you more later in your career than a high salary now?
3. Why do wealthy people often choose jobs where they can learn more instead of jobs where they can earn more?
4. How can working in a small business or a startup help you become more versatile?
5. What are the long-term benefits of working to learn?
6. Why is it important to network during your work experiences?
7. How does gaining sales experience help you in your later career?
8. What is the difference between investing in yourself and working for a paycheck?
9. What are the disadvantages of focusing solely on making money instead of learning?
10. Which choice would you make: a well-paid job or a learning experience?

In the next chapter, we will discuss how you can use the skills and knowledge you have gained to invest in your future and actively start building your financial freedom!

Chapter 6

Lesson 6: The Power of Companies, Taxes and debt

<u>The biggest secret of the rich: being smart with businesses.</u>

When people talk about wealth, they often think it's all about how much money you make. But one of the biggest secrets to wealth isn't how much you make, it's how much you keep. How you handle your taxes and manage your money can make a huge difference. This is one reason why wealthy people often own businesses: they understand how to use tax rules to their advantage to keep more money and grow their wealth.

In this chapter, you'll learn the difference between working for a salary and owning your own business. We'll look at how taxes play a role in wealth, and why wealthy people own businesses to pay less tax and have more control over their finances.

What's the Difference Between a Job and a Business?

When you work for a salary, for example for an employer, you often spend a large portion of your income on **taxes**. Every time you get paid, a significant percentage of your salary goes to the government. This is the standard tax that everyone who works for an employer must pay. You may be making a good amount of money, but these taxes often leave you with much less than you would like.

On the other hand, if you own a **business**, the story is very different. Instead of paying taxes on everything you earn right away, you can deduct many of your business expenses from your profits before you pay taxes. This means that you can spend money on things you need for your business – like materials, equipment, or even travel – and pay less in taxes because these expenses are taken out of your profits.

Rich people understand this difference and use businesses to reduce their tax burden. They know that by owning a business, you have much more control over your finances and how much tax you pay. It's not that they don't pay any taxes at all, but they use the rules to manage their money wisely.

How Do Taxes Work When You Have a Job?

When you work for an employer, a portion of your salary is immediately withheld for taxes before you even see the money. This is done through payroll taxes. The percentage of tax you pay depends on how much you earn, but the more you earn, the more tax you often have to pay. You have little control over how much tax you pay, because the government decides what percentage of your salary is withheld.

This can be daunting. You work hard, but a large portion of your income goes straight to the government. This is one of the reasons why it is difficult to become truly wealthy through a job alone. You earn money, but the high taxes leave relatively little left to save or invest.

How Do Taxes Work When You Have a Business?

When you have a business, the rules are different. Instead of paying taxes first and then making your expenses, as a business owner you can deduct many business expenses from your income before paying taxes. This means that you can spend money on things you need for your business first, such as a laptop, office supplies or business lunches, and only then pay taxes on what is left.

Let's start with a simple example: say you earn €50,000 a year. Below you can see the difference between earning this with a job or with your own company.

Job		Own Company	
Paycheck	€ 50.000	Revenue	€ 50.000
Taxes	-€ 11.800	Car	-€ 5.400
Income	**€ 38.200**	Cell Phone	-€ 540
		Insurance	-€ 1.200
Car	-€ 5.400	Variable costs	-€ 1.800
Cell Phone	-€ 540	Belastingen	-€ 7.801
Insurance	-€ 1.200	**Profit**	**€ 33.259**
Variable costs	-€ 1.800		

Mortgage	-€ 21.000	Mortgage	-€ 21.000
To spend	**€ 8.260**	**To spend**	**€ 12.259**

As you can see, the amounts are the same on both the left and right sides of the column. Costs for car, mobile, insurance, etc. The difference is that with a job, taxes always come first. This money is deducted directly from your salary. With a company, you can first deduct many costs from your income, so that a lower amount remains, on which tax is levied. So you keep more with your own company, than if you would simply pay payroll tax on your entire income. In this example, that advantage is: € 3,999 per year. This gives you more freedom and flexibility in how you use your money.

Why Do Rich People Own Companies?

Rich people know that by owning a company they can manage their money smarter. They can exercise more control over how much tax they pay and how they spend their money. In addition, companies offer other advantages:

- **Tax deduction for business expenses** – As mentioned earlier, business owners can spend money on business expenses and deduct them from their income. This reduces their taxable profit and therefore how much tax they have to pay.
- **Investments in Growth** – Businesses can use their profits to invest in growth, such as buying new equipment, hiring employees, or expanding into new markets. These investments help businesses grow larger and more profitable without paying taxes on all of their income up front.
- **Building Wealth Within a Business** – Business owners can use their businesses to buy assets, such as real estate or stocks, and grow their wealth. Because businesses often pay less tax on profits and investments than individuals, wealthy people can build more wealth through their businesses.
- **Protecting Wealth** – In many cases, owning a business also provides legal protection. Having your wealth in a business can protect you from personal liability in the event of problems or debts.

So wealthy people use businesses as a **vehicle** to build wealth, reduce their tax burden, and secure their financial future.

Your Choice: Working for a Salary or Starting a Business?
Now that you understand the difference between working for a salary and owning a business, you have an important choice to make. Do you continue to work for an employer and accept the high tax burden? Or start your own small business, where you have more control over your income and can take advantage of tax benefits?

Of course, this doesn't mean you have to start a big business right away. You can start small, for example by setting up a side hustle alongside your current job. This could be a small business where you sell something, provide a service, or offer products online. The most important thing is that you learn how businesses work and how to be smart about tax rules.

How to Start a Small Business
Starting a business may seem intimidating, but it doesn't have to be difficult. Here are some simple steps to get started:
1. **Choose an Idea** – Think about something you enjoy doing or are good at. This could be anything from selling handmade goods to offering a service to setting up an online store.
2. **Start Small** – Start a small business alongside your current job. This gives you the chance to experiment without risking all of your income right away.
3. **Learn About Taxes** – Talk to an accountant or research how taxes work for small businesses. This will help you understand how to take advantage of tax benefits.
4. **Use Your Business to Learn** – Running a small business is a great way to learn about finance, marketing, customer service, and more. These skills will not only benefit your business, but your personal finances as well.
5. **Invest in Growth** – As your business grows, you can use the money you earn to grow it further. This can ultimately lead to more profits and greater financial freedom.

The Big Difference Between Good Debt and Bad Debt
The middle class, as we said, earns enough to live comfortably, but they often use their money to buy things they want or need, like a fat bike, a scooter, a car, a house, or a new phone. They often borrow money to pay for those things. We call this "debt." But there are two types of debt: good debt and bad debt.

Bad debt is when you borrow money to buy things that only cost you money and don't increase in value. Think of buying an expensive car or new gadgets on credit. It may seem fun, but in the end you keep paying money for something that decreases in value and doesn't make you any money. This is what many people in the middle class do.

Good debt, on the other hand, is when you borrow money to buy something that helps you make more money. For example, if you borrow money to start a business or invest in something that increases in value, like real estate. This is what rich people often do. They use debt as a tool to make even more money, instead of buying something that costs money.

So the difference is: middle-class people often use **bad debt** to buy things that make them happy in the short term, but rich people use **good debt** to make their money work for them and get richer.

The Big Lesson: Businesses and Good Debt Are the Key to Money
This chapter shows that businesses are a powerful way to lower your tax burden and grow your wealth. Working for a salary limits how much you can keep, but starting a business gives you more control over your finances. Rich people use this strategy to protect and grow their wealth.

Tax rules are there for everyone, but the rich know how to use them to their advantage. By learning how businesses work and how tax rules work, you can use the same strategies to become more financially independent.

Chapter 6 Summary
In this chapter, you learned about the difference between working for a salary and owning a business. Salaries are heavily taxed, while businesses have many tax benefits, such as deducting business expenses. Wealthy people often own businesses because they understand how to use tax rules to their advantage and grow their wealth.

You also learned that starting a small business can be a smart way to start building financial independence. Businesses offer more flexibility in how you manage your money and can help you earn more and pay less taxes in the long run.

Good Debt vs. Bad Debt
- **Bad Debt:** Borrowing money for consumption, such as expensive cars or gadgets, that depreciate in value and do not provide additional income.
- **Good Debt:** Borrowing money to invest in something that helps you generate more income, such as real estate or a business.

The Important Lesson
This chapter emphasizes that businesses and the strategic use of good debt are crucial to building wealth. By understanding the rules around taxes and business, you can become more financially independent and protect and grow your wealth. Wealthy people know how to use these strategies to secure their financial future.

Questionnaire

1. Why do people with jobs often pay more in taxes than people who own a business?
2. What are some tax benefits of owning a business?
3. Why do wealthy people often choose to own businesses instead of just earning a salary?
4. What is the difference between paying taxes on your salary and paying taxes on your business income?
5. How can you start a small business while still working your current job?
6. What are some business expenses you can deduct when you own a business?
7. Why is it important to learn about tax rules when you own a business?
8. How can owning a business help protect your wealth?
9. What are the benefits of investing in the growth of your business?
10. What step would you take to start building your own business?

In the next chapter, we'll dive deeper into how to make your money work for you so you can become financially independent!

The Obstacles to Your First Million

The big difference between a rich person and a
poor person is how they deal with fear

Everyone wants to be successful, but not everyone achieves that success. This is not only due to a lack of knowledge or opportunities, but often due to the obstacles we face on the road to financial freedom. These obstacles can be within ourselves: our **fears**, **doubts**, **bad behavior**, and sometimes even our **arrogance**. In this chapter, we will discuss the five biggest obstacles that can hold you back on your path to wealth and, more importantly, how to overcome them.

Rich people also have these obstacles, but they learn how to deal with them. If you learn how to recognize and overcome these obstacles, you will take another step towards financial freedom.

1. Fear: The Biggest Enemy of Success

Fear is something that everyone deals with, especially when it comes to money. We are afraid of losing money, afraid of making mistakes, and sometimes even afraid of success because we don't know what to expect. These fears often keep people trapped in a safe, but limited situation. They are afraid to take risks or try new things because they are afraid of failure.

But here's the reality: **everyone fails**. The difference between successful people and those who aren't is that successful people learn from their mistakes instead of being afraid. Rich people take controlled risks because they understand that sometimes you have to fail to learn and grow.

How to Overcome Fear

The only way to overcome fear is to go through it. Instead of letting the possibility of failure scare you, use that fear as motivation to be better prepared. Start small, take calculated risks, and learn from every step you take. Making mistakes is part of life; it's what you learn from them that matters.

2. Cynicism: Questioning Everything

Cynicism is the tendency to doubt everything and always see the negative. Cynical people say things like, "That won't work," or "Only rich people can do that." They think success is for other people, not them. This kind of thinking prevents you from taking action, even when opportunities are right in front of you.

Many people become cynical because they have been disappointed in the past, perhaps because of failures or bad experiences. But if you always distrust everything, you will never seize the opportunities that can help you move forward.

How do you overcome cynicism?

Learn to be open to possibilities. Instead of immediately thinking that something won't work, ask yourself, "How can I make this work for me?" Try new things with an open mind and see what happens. Be curious instead of skeptical, and you will find that there are more opportunities than you thought.

3. Laziness: Procrastination and Doing Nothing

Laziness can be a major obstacle on the road to success. Sometimes it's easier to sit back, watch Netflix, or scroll through social media instead of taking action. We often think, "I'll do it tomorrow." But the truth is that tomorrow often never comes, and procrastination ends up costing us dearly.

Rich people understand that success requires action. They know that even small, daily steps will bring them closer to their goals. The difference between rich and non-rich people is often simply that rich people have the discipline to keep taking action.

How to overcome laziness

The best way to overcome laziness is to break your goals down into small, manageable tasks. Make a plan and take one step toward your goal every day. Even if it's just 15 minutes, you'll notice that you're making progress. The key is consistency: keep doing something every day, even if it seems small.

4. Bad Habits: Impulsive Spending

Bad habits, like **impulsive spending**, can sabotage your financial success. You may recognize this: you walk through the store and see something you don't need, but buy it anyway because it looks nice. Or you see a sale online and you immediately spend your money without thinking. These types of expenses quickly add up and can prevent you from saving or investing.

Wealthy people have control over their habits. They don't just spend their money, but take the time to think about their purchases and invest in things that will make them richer in the long run.

How do you overcome bad habits?
Learn to make conscious choices. Every time you want to buy something, ask yourself: "Do I really need this? And does this add value to my life?" Create a budget and stick to it. By being more conscious with your money, you can avoid impulsive purchases and save more for investments that will grow your wealth.

5. Arrogance: Thinking You Know It All
One of the most dangerous obstacles to success is **arrogance**. This happens when you think you know everything and that you don't need to learn anything more. People who are arrogant stop seeking new knowledge and opportunities, and often get stuck in the same patterns. They ignore valuable advice and get stuck because they are not open to growth.

Rich people know that you never stop learning. They are always looking for ways to improve themselves, learn new things, and expand their knowledge. They understand that the world is constantly changing and that they must change with it to remain successful.

How to overcome arrogance
The best way to overcome arrogance is to always remain a **learner**. Ask questions, seek new information, and don't be afraid to ask for advice from people who know more than you. The more you know, the better you can make financial decisions and the more opportunities you can take advantage of.

Understanding and Managing Risks
Rich people aren't afraid to take risks, but they take smart risks that can make them more money in the long run. The difference is that they think carefully about the potential consequences and find ways to mitigate the

risks. They do this by doing their research, consulting with experts, or only investing in things they understand well.

Why is this important?
Many people avoid taking risks because they're afraid of losing money. But taking risks is an important part of becoming successful. Without taking risks, it's hard to seize opportunities that can help you grow financially. The key is to not just take risks, but to learn how to manage them. You do this by being well prepared, making smart choices, and sometimes learning from mistakes.

How can you apply this?
As a teenager, you can start understanding and managing risks by taking small steps. For example, before you spend money on something big, research whether it's worth it. If you are planning to invest in something (like stocks or a small project), make sure you learn enough about how it works first.

Another example is starting a small business. This can be a risk because it may not be successful right away, but by preparing well and taking the time to learn, you can reduce this risk and learn a lot at the same time.

How wealthy people manage risk:
- **Research:** They fully understand what they are investing in before they spend money.
- **Diversify:** They spread their investments so that if one thing fails, they don't lose everything.
- **Consult experts:** They work with financial advisors, accountants, or other experts to make the best decisions.

Lesson for you: Taking risks is not something to be afraid of, as long as you know how to do it wisely. By gathering the right information, considering your options, and sometimes spreading your risks, you can learn to manage risk and even use it to your advantage.

Your Choice: How Will You Handle the Obstacles?
Now that you know these five obstacles and how to manage the risks, it is time to think about how you deal with them. Which of these obstacles do you recognize in yourself? Do you suffer from fear of failure? Are you sometimes too cynical or lazy? Or do you notice that you have impulsive habits that hold you back?

This is the time to decide how you deal with these obstacles. Are you going to recognize and overcome them, or are you going to let them get in your way? The choices you make will determine whether or not you can become successful with money.

Chapter 7 Summary

The difference between rich and poor people lies in how they deal with fear and other obstacles on the road to financial freedom. Success is not only dependent on knowledge or opportunity, but also on overcoming internal barriers such as fear, cynicism, laziness, bad habits, and arrogance. Rich people learn to deal with these obstacles, which helps them achieve financial success.

Overcoming Obstacles

In this chapter, you learned about the five biggest obstacles to success with money: fear, cynicism, laziness, bad habits, and arrogance. These obstacles can hold you back if you don't recognize and address them. Rich people have these obstacles too, but they learn how to deal with them to move forward.

By being conscious about your mindset and habits, you can overcome these obstacles and pave your path to financial freedom. Success is not only about knowledge and opportunity, but also about how you deal with the mental barriers that come your way.

Understanding and Managing Risks

Wealthy people take calculated risks that can help them grow financially. They understand that risks are an essential part of success, if managed properly.

Questionnaire

1. What is your biggest fear when it comes to money, and how can you overcome it?
2. How do you recognize cynicism in yourself? And how can it stop you from seeing opportunities?
3. When do you notice that you are lazy, and what can you do to take action?
4. What bad habits do you have when it comes to spending money? How can you change them?
5. Have you ever felt like you know it all? How can this limit your growth?
6. What can you do to remain a conscious learner and always learn new things?
7. How can you take small, daily steps to overcome laziness?
8. What could you do today to break a bad financial habit?
9. What is an example of a risk you can take to overcome your fear?
10. What is one action you can take to overcome one of these obstacles?

In the next chapter, we will delve deeper into how you can make your first investment and actively build your financial future!

Chapter 8

Getting Started

Congratulations! You've learned a lot about money, investing, and how to get rich in the past few chapters. But here's the most important lesson: wealth isn't just about having a lot of money. It starts with **how you think**. Your mindset determines the choices you make, how you deal with obstacles, and ultimately whether you'll succeed. This final chapter is about developing a **wealth mindset**, a way of thinking that will help you succeed in your financial life—and beyond.

Rich people think differently about money. They see opportunities where others see problems. They continue to learn, even after they've achieved success. They take responsibility for their own financial future, and that's exactly what you can do. Let's explore how you can develop this mindset together.

What is a Wealth Mindset?

A wealth mindset is a way of thinking that focuses on growth, learning, and making smart financial decisions. People with this mindset aren't afraid to take risks because they know that mistakes make them stronger. They believe that they are in control of their own financial success, and that through smart investments, hard work, and continuous learning, they can build wealth.

It's like sports: if you want to be a top athlete, you have to train every day, even when you're tired. You have to persevere, even when you lose, because you know that only through hard work and dedication can you win. The same goes for money: you have to keep learning, even when you make mistakes, and always try to get better at managing your money.

Why is this mindset important?

The way you think about money can have a big impact on your financial success. If you believe that there are enough opportunities for everyone and that you can shape your own future, you're much more likely to take risks and try new things. This often leads to better results, while a mindset focused on scarcity and limitations can hold you back and prevent you from taking advantage of your opportunities.

How can you apply this mindset?
Here are a few ways to develop a wealthy mindset:
- **Focus on opportunities:** Learn to view situations from the perspective of opportunities rather than problems. Ask yourself, "What can I learn from this situation?" or "How can I solve this problem?" instead of thinking it's not possible.
- **Surround yourself with positive influences:** Spend time with people who have a positive and successful mindset. This can help you think more positively and gain new ideas.
- **Invest in yourself:** Keep learning and growing. This can be done by reading books, taking classes, or finding mentors. The more you know, the more opportunities you can see and seize.
- **Set goals:** Set clear, achievable goals for yourself. This will help you stay focused on what you want to achieve and encourage you to take action to achieve those goals.

Lesson for you:
Your mindset has a huge impact on your financial future. By learning to think like wealthy people and see opportunities rather than limitations, you can put yourself in a position to seize opportunities and improve your financial situation.

The Power of Positive Thinking
One of the most important qualities of a wealth mindset is **positive thinking**. This doesn't mean that you should always be happy or never doubt yourself, but that you believe that you have possibilities and that you are capable of achieving financial freedom. People with a positive mindset don't think, "I can't do that," but ask themselves, **"How can I make this happen?"**

To translate this to money, change your thoughts from "I can't afford that" to "How can I afford this?" Instead of focusing on what isn't possible, they look for solutions. This way of thinking helps them not get stuck in problems, but instead look for opportunities. Positive thinking is one of the most powerful forces you can use to develop your wealth mindset.

Learn from Your Mistakes

Everyone makes mistakes, especially when it comes to money. You might buy something you don't need, or make a bad financial decision. But people with a wealth mindset don't let these mistakes discourage them. They see mistakes as opportunities to learn. Instead of saying, "I failed," they say, **"What can I learn from this situation?"**

Developing a wealth mindset means seeing mistakes as part of your learning process. Rich people have often made more mistakes than unsuccessful people because they were willing to take risks and learn from what went wrong. Making mistakes is okay, as long as you learn from them and move on.

How can you learn from mistakes?

Here are some ways to develop this mindset:
- **Reflect on your mistakes:** Take time to think about what went wrong and why. What could you have done differently? This will help you identify and understand the lessons learned.
- **Don't be afraid to take risks:** Try new things, even if they are scary. It's better to fail and learn than never to try at all.
- **Ask for feedback:** Talk to others about your experiences and ask for their opinions. This can help you gain new insights and improve your approach.
- **Stay persistent:** Don't let setbacks discourage you. Most successful people have made countless mistakes before reaching their goals. What matters is that you keep trying.

Lesson for you:

It's okay to make mistakes, especially on your financial journey. What's more important is that you learn from them and don't give up. Every step, even the wrong ones, will bring you closer to your goal as long as you're willing to learn and adjust your approach.

Always Keep Learning

A wealth mindset also means that you never stop learning. The world is constantly changing, and there are always new opportunities, technologies, and ways to make money. Wealthy people know this, and that's why they invest in their own knowledge. They read books, take courses, and keep looking for new ways to grow their money.

You may feel like you know everything you need to know about money now, but there is always more to learn. You never know everything. The more you learn about money and investing, the better you can make financial decisions. That's why it's important to always stay curious and keep looking for new ways to expand your knowledge.

Making Smart Financial Decisions

A wealth mindset also means that you make **smart financial decisions**. This means that you don't just spend money on things you don't need, but consciously choose where you spend your money. You think about the long term instead of just the short term. People with a wealth mindset invest their money in assets that will grow their wealth, such as stocks, businesses, or real estate, rather than spending it on liabilities that will actually diminish their money in the long run.

Before making a decision about money, you can always ask yourself, "**Will this help me build wealth?**" If the answer is no, you might want to reconsider that expenditure. Wealthy people prioritize their financial goals and make choices that will move them closer to those goals.

Taking Responsibility for Your Future

The most important thing about a wealth mindset is taking responsibility for your own financial future. This means not waiting for others to take care of it for you, but taking action yourself. People with a wealth mindset know that they are the only ones responsible for their success, and that they have the power to determine their future.

If you start taking responsibility for your money, your spending, and your investments today, you will be ahead of most people. Wealthy people don't wait for luck or random opportunities. They create their own opportunities through hard work, smart decisions, and continuous learning.

Your Choice: Keep Working on Your Mindset?

Now that you've read all the chapters, it's time to think about the future. You've learned a lot about how wealthy people think and how you can adopt their habits to build your own wealth. But the big question is: **what are you going to do now?**

You have two choices:
1. **You keep working on your wealth mindset.** You keep learning, making smart financial decisions, and investing in yourself and your future.
2. **You fall back into old habits.** Maybe you think, "This is too much work," and give up before you even start. Or you think wealth isn't for you and get stuck in old patterns.

Whatever choice you make, you will see the consequences in your life. If you choose a wealth mindset, you will find that over time you will have more opportunities, more control over your money, and ultimately achieve financial freedom. But if you fall back into old habits, you will find yourself continuing to face financial problems.

Create a Financial Plan for Your First Million

Now that you know how important it is to develop a wealth mindset, it's time to create a plan. A financial plan will help you stay focused and achieve your goals.

Here are a few steps to get you started:
1. **Set a goal.** What do you want to achieve? Do you want to save for a big purchase, invest in stocks, or maybe even start your own business? Write down your goals.
2. **Create a budget.** Look at how much money you have coming in and how much you're spending. Decide where you can save and how much you can invest.
3. **Learn something new every day.** Keep reading books, listening to podcasts, and taking courses on money, business, and investing. The more you learn, the better you'll be at making financial decisions.
4. **Stay focused.** It can be hard to keep going at times, but remember that every step you take will bring you closer to your goal.

Pay Yourself First

The principle of "Pay Yourself First" means that every time you receive money, such as your allowance or salary, you put some of that money aside for yourself first, before paying other bills or buying things. This could mean setting aside a percentage of your income for savings or investments. The idea is that you are making sure that your financial future is a priority, before you spend money on other things.

Why is this important?
Many people make the mistake of spending all their money on bills and expenses, and then saving or investing what is left (if there is any at all). This can lead to the idea that there is never enough money to save or invest, because the focus is on spending. By paying yourself first, you ensure that you are actively building wealth and growing your financial base.

How can you apply this?
Here are a few steps to apply the "Pay Yourself First" principle to your life:
1. **Set a percentage:** Decide on a percentage of your income that you want to put aside each time you receive money. This could be 10%, for example. Start with something small if necessary, and increase the percentage as you gain financial flexibility.
2. **Set up a savings or investment account:** Make sure that the money you put aside is separate from your expenses. This could be a savings account for short-term savings or an investment account for long-term investments.
3. **Automate your savings:** If possible, set up automatic transfers so that a portion of your income goes directly into your savings or investment account. This will make it easier to stick to the principle.
4. **Take a look at your spending:** When you create your budget, determine your "pay yourself" amount first, and then see what you have left over for other expenses. This will also help you become more aware of your spending habits.

Lesson for you:
Paying yourself first ensures that you are always working on building your financial future. It doesn't matter how much you earn; if you apply this principle, you will create a habit of saving and investing. This will help you have more financial freedom later on.

Chapter 8 Summary

In this chapter, you learned that wealth starts with a mindset. Wealthy people think differently about money: they make smart decisions, learn from their mistakes, never stop learning, and take responsibility for their future. By adopting this mindset, you too can begin your path to financial freedom.

The choice is yours: will you continue to work on your wealth mindset, or will you fall back into old habits? The path to wealth doesn't start with money, it starts with how you think and the choices you make.

Questionnaire

1. What does a wealth mindset mean to you?
2. How can you think positively and see opportunities instead of problems?
3. How do you deal with mistakes and what can you learn from them?
4. What is an example of a smart financial decision you can make soon?
5. How can you learn something new about money and investing every day?
6. How can you make a financial plan for your future?
7. What is a long-term goal you can set for your finances?
8. How can you take responsibility for your financial future?
9. What could you do today to start developing your wealth mindset?
10. What can you do to keep going, even when things get tough?

These questions will help you organize your thoughts and create a clear plan for your financial future. This is the beginning of your journey to wealth – and it all starts with the right mindset.

Final Thoughts

Now that you've read the key lessons from From Pocket Money to Millionaire, it's time to reflect on what you've learned and how you can apply this knowledge to your own life. This book isn't just about getting rich, it's about how you think about money and how you can make it work for you. The ideas and concepts that Rich Dad taught me go beyond simply making money. They show you how to take control of your financial future by making smart choices and seizing opportunities.

Summary of Key Lessons

- **Wealth Comes from the Right Mindset** – The difference between rich and poor people is primarily in the way they think about money. Rich people make money work for them, while poor people work for money.
- **Invest in Yourself and Your Money Knowledge** – You've learned that understanding the basics of money is the first step to being successful with money. Never stop learning, because the more you know, the better you can manage your money.
- **Take Action** – The most important thing is not how much you know, but what you do with that knowledge. It doesn't matter if you start small, as long as you take action and learn from your experiences.
- **Overcome your fears and doubts** – Fear and doubt can hold you back, but by challenging yourself and not letting fear paralyze you, you can grow and achieve your goals.
- **Be patient and consistent** – Building wealth takes time. It's not a sprint, it's a marathon. By consistently taking small steps and sticking to your plan, you can slowly but surely achieve financial success.

Take control of your future

The most important thing you can take away from this book is that you are the master of your own financial future. The choices you make now will impact your life later. Whether you choose to learn more about money, invest, or make smart financial decisions, it all starts with action.

Every day, you can choose to improve your financial skills and learn from your mistakes. Start small, be patient, and never stop learning. By adopting this mindset, you can not only achieve financial freedom, but also gain more control over your life and make your dreams come true.

So, what's your next step? Start now – take what you've learned and put it into action.